rel[am]ent

rel[am]ent

POEMS

Jamison Crabtree

WINNER OF THE 2014 WASHINGTON PRIZE

THE WORD WORKS
WASHINGTON, D.C.

Cover design: Susan Pearce Design
Author photograph: Jamison Crabtree
Cover art: "Stop," T.J. Scott, photograph.

LCCN: 2014952561
ISBN: 978-0-915380-92-3

Acknowledgments

I am grateful to the editors of the journals in which versions of these poems have appeared:

The Ampersand Review, Anti-, apt, Blackbird, Colorado Review, DIAGRAM, Hawai'i Review, >kill author, Makeout Creek, No Tell Motel, The Offending Adam, PANK, and *Toad.*

Thanks to my family, friends, students, and teachers for their incredible kindness; especially to Andrea and Drew Burk, Zach Buscher, Aaric Callahan, Mary Chen, Matthew John Conley, Ben Gelisan, Bryan Helm, Lauren Leggett, George Life, Chris Litton, Richard Siken, Lily Trave, Christina Vega-Westhoff, Meg Wade, and my parents for their support and help with the book. Also, an enormous thank you to the judges, editors, and readers at The Word Works who made this book possible, especially Nancy White.

Special thanks to Carleen Tibbetts and Marilyn McCabe for their work copyediting this book.

Many of these poems would never have been possible without access to the following places, all of which I feel especially indebted to: The Byrd Theater, Casa Video, The Loft, The University of Arizona Poetry Center, and Hotel Congress.

CONTENTS

In memory of [   ]

WE HAVE REASON TO BE AFRAID.
THIS IS A TERRIBLE PLACE.

❧

I SAW A LIGHT BUT DID NOT KNOW WHERE IT WAS HEADED.

❧

IT'S ALIVE. IT'S ALIVE.

LAMENT

Everywhere,

someone has spoken of their dead lover, everywhere someone
expects an audience and the proper applause. If you could stand

somewhere dramatic enough; where the words wind down
from the cliffs and waves lap at the names of lost children,

where the moon shows its face in the daylight, naked,
without the makeup of night,
where the clamor of the rains against a canopy of elms
sounds remarkably similar to the clamor of rain

against the flat paddles of prickly pears; where the stories you hear
start to sound natural, start to sound as your own, to feel as your own: then,
then, the act of lamenting would be dignified. So try it:
this *listening*. Mistake thunder

for ultimatum, the disagreements of the sea

for language. What you hear must come

from somewhere — a whisper, or a spirit,
a neighbor raising their voice and talking to themselves
or the wrong pills in one of your little red plastic bottles. Either everything

speaks or nothing

speaks or something else entirely. Anyone could talk to themselves
and say they've heard the voice of angels; all of this majesty
is terrifying. And if the world goes quiet,

be assured that something terrible has happened.

The world can bear with itself; like us,
it must only turn

inward and announce. Call the shivers of crickets a music —

the trigs' timbal, the screams of moths, the mangy wails
that flood the bushes: call it *melody*. Babies cry

in order to get your attention: to say *something is wrong here.*

Awe-struck or dumbstruck, what we can't comprehend
bludgeons us.

Because our suffering,
in all its grotesque dazzle, is terrible

because it's manageable. Because we can live with this,
because we've been doing it for so long already.

lament for dr. frankenstein

There is no word for digging in the rain,
but it should have a wet sound to it. For us,

the act of creation is like doing the foxtrot with crutches

except I would not crush your toes, you'd crush mine,
and together we'd have a miserable sort of grace. For the sound,

sledging, maybe?

None of my birdhouses, bookends, or recipes
have hated me for making them, though once

the tail of a paper tiger slit the skin beneath my pinkynail.
I think it was an accident. Victor,
I like the structure of dance.

And my apologies, but we need
to compare the interpretation of grief

to grief itself. The beautiful girl who works the register

at the piggly wiggly tells me, each time I go to buy my milk
and my whatchamacallits and my plumcots and grapples,

that beauty is dead
and because I believe her

when she says she has suffered
more than I have, I distrust everything she says.

But she may be right.

What I'm saying, Victor, is that no one ever listened to you
for the same reason that no one ever listens: you can't trust a person in pain
to decide what's best for themselves.

Since this is our dance, let's cut the bullshit:
when it comes to you,
there are two things I regret, these:

and *one*:
if you were dumber, you'd never have been a monster

and *two*:
you could never have been any dumber.

And *three*, and *turn*.

lament for the creature from the black lagoon

Amphibian-men do not frighten me
unless they're holding something — violins especially.

I heard my father play the violin but

only once, *col legno*;
he made a switch of the bow and performed the song of the body

splintering itself. And after: if the creature from the black lagoon
emerged from his depths playing a perfectly tuned fiddle,

I would reluctantly nod in appreciation of the skill
but not the music. I would need to reevaluate my life

because I have a secret.

Which is this: even if, scientifically speaking, I am not, I feel
more important than the creature from the black lagoon,

especially with his horse-wide eyes, his unnecessarily finned head,
with that dumb capon comb rising back.

Monsters everywhere have learned to make instruments
out of women

and they play the same dull note
until the throat goes raw.

Another secret:

appalachia houses hundreds of monsters
all living in seclusion, chopping wood
beside their cabins (I know,

my father is from that area).

sunset, no sun

To place the sun is to provide a sky; like a page, it's what's printed there that makes us bawl. A blank. My great-great-great-great-great-great-grandson once told me something about how I didn't even recognize him anymore. I told him *I never didn't*. Sorry for texting you that last night, sorry for my drunk letters, drunk telegrams, sorry for the pie-eyed carrier pigeons cooing outside your windowsill at 3:24 in the morning. I'm just scared that the language won't wait; and I miss you.

Be assured, your photos of the letter in ash, the melted phone, the roasted pigeon all reached me. Thank you. The sun reads whatever burns, did you know that? It knows the dirtiest books and the endless tale of garbage, the black snaking up and away. *But bucko*, you say, *this story needs a cardo*. A cold cherry coke and a pack of rainbow-colored cigarettes. A gun that no one's afraid of, that we shoot with, at cans, for fun, and that never hurts anyone, anywhere, ever. But if I gave that to you, this story could never end. So here is the gun you asked for: take it, take it as a kindness.

lament for dracula

The mist thought itself a man, the man thought himself

down to the thin; woke damp, woke

dim, symmetric and dumbstrung across the tobacco rows
of ivor, virginia. Pink flowers to trouble the hair; pink flowers
to fret empty the lungs. What has begun began

with a drunk firing a frog gig, navigating swamplands
by muzzleflash. She named the shots
stars. Next, came you,

you to carve ghosts into bus-stop benches.
You, to cry into the barrel of your guns.

We can live forever among our wrong loves

if we can grieve, if we believe we are capable

of any real grief (no, we are not). Trace a name
beneath the black plate of the moon:

your secret constellations,
try to share them with anyone and you'll never aim at the right spot.
So plot their ecliptics for yourself. Track their unluster. The man

thought itself a mist and so thought it could know itself

by what it filled, by what encircled it.

And so it disappeared. If you're alive, it's because the heart
is a smaller target than you'd think.

lament for count orlok

Fog-risen, night-spurned, and star-addled: the milkman
is the last true enemy of the morning. The milkman

who is no one; milkman-two-steps-
ahead-of-you, milkman-who-

casts-his-shadow-against-your-bedroom-window,

milkman-who-approaches-your-door-while-you-sleep, who never knocks.

Even as the lonesomely alonesome stars
drag their terrible quiet behind them,
you can never be as alone as you feel.

Good Count, gentle
Count, to see the bottles arrive
would be to unravel the last myth of the old country.

Let's unravel it, let's make believe; let's play,

let's say we didn't come from out a bog or swamp, not from out

the desert or hell or even a suburb of louisville, kentucky,
where all the suicides are declared accidents

out of a sense of common decency. Count,

pretend you were

born to exist in the private moments of the world,
alongside those other secreted works: of the baker, the hungry owl,

the newspaper boy riding his bike at dawn, the newspaper man driving
his ford with the radio tuned to static.
But silly you, silly-billy you, you lit out for the first bare neck

you saw a photograph of,
and no one could blame you for that. Beauty enchants us all to cinders.

We cross oceans every day out of simple desperation. And yes,

I'm suspicious of you now; how can anyone be of use
to someone while troubling them? I'm suspicious

that you knew, all along, what most of us suspected;
when we will allow beauty to end us,
it so rarely does.

how not to be lonely

Refuse to be found. Start with your phone; leave it on silent, facing south,
someplace forgettable — behind the ice cube trays in the freezer

or underneath the bathroom sink, behind the poisons and soaps:

wheresoever you never
go, so you can never be

sure whether everyone you've ever met
is calling you to tell you that they miss
or forgive or thank or care for you. Start to trust

that the voices of your friends
are everywhere, even if you can't hear them.

So long as you don't speak to anyone, so long

as you don't see anyone, this could always be happening. Instead,

lug yourself out into the night and listen —
for the unabashed weeping of insects, for the
nightclouds scrubbing the light along the chill. Listen

for the footfalls of all those furry little animals
that don't need to love

anything, but yet call out to the moon or to the stars

or whatever it is
that they can't see. They're calling out to the silence;

be the silence that answers.

lament for the man who changed his mind

Let's forget our lives. Let's start at each birth and work our way back,
out of the screaming. I gave up

my body to whatever would let me forget it
and I woke up with thirty-seven scars.

Each with its own unique story: this one I was born with
(and yes, the rest as well). Unhinge the skull and place your brain
into my body. Together, let us say something eloquent,
like the graceful *fuck-it*. That's it,

the phrase to say. It begins with profanity
and ends with the world looking gorgeous from any pair of eyes.

How unfair is that? (Very unvery) in your body,
I think I would know the difference between
vase and vase. I would stand in front of a tall mirror

and make my pecs dance. I would share it through the internet.

I want to steal your gangly arms, your open face;
leave my own as offal and untouchable.

What I want is to comb your hair with your fingers.

The history of the skeleton
is one of carelessness; the bones are careless
with the muscle, the muscle insouciant with the skin.

So. Give me yours.

lament for the fly

Curse the inevitable coincidence; curse
the moment and Andre, curse those loyal to it! Curse it all.

Like when you find cheerwine
in a gas station right after you remember that you haven't
seen it anywhere since your son died or like

when you find an old letter in the wheel well of your trunk

when all you needed was a tire. Andre,

the past is useless, I need to know
why I'm doing what I'm doing

now because I'm afraid to deal
with the things I've done (I am missing
the tip-top-bit of my right thumb; I am a garden of bruises). No.

I meant I'm afraid to recall all
that I couldn't bring myself to do.

Do you have any clue what I mean? Let's agree

to share our memories, puddle them together,
so we can say of your lost hand, of your lost head,

that they were *crushed*. And that was all.

Andre, do your fingers miss your hand;
does your head miss your neck? There are so many people
that miss what they didn't appreciate. Andre, we share what

we share (what do we
share?). Frankly, *we* aren't necessary. There is a girl

and she tells me she conceived my son
like an idea, to lose, like a daydream. And *poof.*

It's how it goes. We were born
out of trauma; so it makes sense that we live through it.

And Andre, I am thankful for all
that I can manage to forget.

lament for freddy krueger

This is the room without
a view; where we build a fire and keep it

as a window. The room
where we forget birthdays
and middle names and where the shampoo

that once made someone else's hair smell
so nice is no longer being manufactured.

This is the room where the days slant by
and hours turn into residue
souring the walls. Where our desires are

final and finally our own
because we no longer have a need for anything. This is the hidden room,

the room under the ground with the door nailed shut.
The room where we trace our names
across the ceilings and the walls

and wait for them to bloom.

Mr. K— , there is a dream I have, where out of his naval uniform,
donald duck appears, naked as snow,

and explains why everyone will eventually
abandon me (he says it happens

because I expect it to, *so why shouldn't it?*

he says *quack quack quack?*). And it makes no sense
because awake, I can never understand a damned lick
of what he says. And the dream somehow seems less ridiculous

than the reasons I have for waddling

through the days. Less fantastic
than taking out the trash or pulling hair out of the drain.

Mr. K— , life is too boring to fathom (I must say so).

And we were made for rest. You, who replaced his fingers
with razors, will injure
whatever you try to protect

unless you are very, very careful. And no one is that careful,
so hold me. O, tightly.

we shouldn't be left; lone or alonely; outside of rooms

; are other rooms and stone; ruin and cheap and cheaper likker and even cheaper-er liqueurs; with pictures on the bottle of someone's lost child; have you seen; my baby baby baby boy; no; lah; then look harder; when we couldn't find one we made one; but she mistook a stranger's handsome tongue for my own; but the baby was fumbled; but the moon was pear-shaped and unloved; but you've missed the point; I knew as soon as she took her necklace from around her neck and placed it beside the bed that it was your monozygotic twin; when my lap is cold I miss the snaggletoothed cat who lived there for five scotched years; the one who jumped into the rain from the second story window; alas; I was never seen again; but that happened when the inside was escapable if only momentarily; now; the door; it only locks from the outside; and when the sun comes in through the window I know that it is still outside of the window; it's the same with us; I know that somewhere someone is on their knees praying; not because they're humble; but because they're too tired to stand up to do it;

lament for the body snatchers

Sugarcube, darling me-but-not-me,
I am waiting to dissolve

into the well prepared bed
wearing my suit and my finest pearls.

I'm long sick of being me, of this awful they (this awful

day). Keep me company. Stay

and have a drink. Wait until the stars appear
(powdered sugar
on a long black cake) before you go. Me-who-

is-not, me: it's time to give up
on the body; give up

on those fat bags of secrets bound to burst.

They are worth less than you think
(I did not want to be me). But you won't
and you don't

listen. You, crippled by sincerity, you
are as handsome as hd tv
(as copy, darling).

And maybe you shouldn't listen.

Check the source and such. I regularly mistake

anteros for eros, hephaestus for my father, the new
yorker for the new york times.

Stranger, starling, *sugarcube*, I keep my face
bruised; wear it delicately.

lament for the mother of sighs

Call out into the walls, into the empty pipes
until you manage to dislocate your voice (like a bone)
from your lungs.

Because I was too ugly to make myself invisible, I kept quiet.
If you press your silhouette into the bed

you can lay yourself down beside it. You can wait

for someone to come back
from the other room, with a glass
of milk and a story about a windy day,

to kiss you goodnight. Your sobbing
fell strangely through the building, like flour
sifted onto an apple pie. Like the cracked insulation

that leaks from the ceiling
and betrays the footsteps of the upstairs neighbor:

I am covered in your sobbing.

When you said your heart was steel, I believed you.

I wanted to melt it,
to fashion myself some bolts or a diver's helmet, maybe,
with what was there. It's a feeling — it (isn't) doesn't matter. But it could be
something to keep with me, for me to take, and to be gone.

lament for the incredible melting man

Steve! No: Astro-Steve; O! I believe
that if we felt whole, maybe we could
control ourselves. Maybe me, snow-bound me,

shoeless me, who stands outside appalachian cabins
building snow families only to watch them
shrink, could feel complete and done and finished.

That would be nice.

Astro-Steve, no one said we had to live
with the hand we're dealt (we can die or better

yet, we can fix ourselves).

I couldn't fix myself
and I am still alive (but have I fortified myself
with drugs and sex and booze and vice,

O Steve! life can be so, O Steve, so nice). So spaceman, please,

know that there are other options too.

Even if your children don't remember to call you on your birthday
and your wife never recognizes your cheeks
after you shave, you needn't worry.

Remember, you went impossibly up and we, here,
still waved to what we couldn't see
from mountains, from steeples, from the tops of trees,

from behind arcade machines, from the quantum of our lives.
And when you returned,
we all still looked like toys. Steve,

I started a fire with a match
and Steve, remember, even the tiny things we build to keep us warm
are capable of destroying us.

to prevent pain

Cause pain. Be first, be fast. Oh yes — at last a way to strip the desperate from the landscape; a way to put yourself back into it. To kiss me would be cruel.

So kiss me and wake to the mice that startle the brush; to someone who kneels down to touch your lips with a finger; then with their own faint mouth.

But there were neither hips nor skin, not even your own — there was a tree and the tree and the night were tressed, all knotted and gnarled with stars.

Tonight, the forest is empty of its little prey; they dine at the feet of the cities, hunters feather the trees. There are no fingertips to slender the constellations from the branches. No callused sky.

And so you want to die but if you want to die, you won't. *But you will you will you will* calls out the owl. Calls out the owl to the tiny wild.

[AM]

Awe makes for such a sloppy musick,
so choose whether to murmur the low ooos and AHHs or

to beat at the pig-iron we call our sorrows
until we've hewn a pile of rough arias; the arias
in which our voice portends the carbon dusk.

We are here to unsoothe the world. Take this sledgehammer

and mend your life. Ours too, because our grief is shared — like sweetbutter
or disease it spreads, and our joys

are only interesting if they involve our vanity or sex or injury.

We can no longer speak for ourselves so pour us
something dark to drink. Poor us,

with our champagne flute of night; with our stars
bubbling and popping; with our nervous lovers

who wake without knowing whether to leave quietly or to leave silently.

Oh, poor us, we shouldn't be so dramatic, yes, yes-yes, we are condemned,
deserted; oh alas or ach or lah!: *so what?*

Look at the spaces you touch: did you not see this coming?

With your mismatched silver
in the kitchen drawers, with the people you place in the ground, with
the lost intimacies of toothbrushes and bobby pins and toiletries

that all change with each new love you let into your house. Each person

you meet takes you further and further away from the ones you'll meet later.
We were never a safe place for what we keep inside; we could never

shelter each other. Your losses are permanent and bound by words.
Dead children are searching for you.

They drag their broken limbs behind them and tear at their blue dresses,
their pink shirts. They are coming to

you, for you. From out of the red forests, the ants herald their arrival.

From suburban reservoirs, little boys
bloat their way back towards the surface
and climb to the banks dripping blind.

From along the abandoned highways, sticky with tar, they, heatwet,
coruscate; behind every camber they're rising up: they're coming for you.

And our skeletons, they smile like children;
they give away the secret:

we remain children. So be careful. We are coming for us.

golem

I.

So speak. So I

      speak to you; measure
      by snake scale the story
      we call name

Until we can see a pattern, den-born
      and squirming, through the witchgrass.

To tell it is to rattle;
it is to split it   open   down the belly,
                 to expose
the space between each wall. Our unformed spirits

amount to breath
      slithering out, into the snow.

II.

I am jealous.
The animals implicate their presence
         with such obvious subtlety.

Their dim rustle,   their calls that
                        blanket the wood.

The payphone
out behind smalltownburgville drug and grocery

        howls all night   like a child
waiting to be grabbed by its scruff
and deposited in a crib.

I ask a favor of you, you, you:
        harvest the scraps of my voice—
sew them into a scarf; anything

to wrap a face in, to hold
heat, candle sure.
The countryside's a song
growing bars one tree at a time.

Keep this quarter for the call.

III.

The forest snickers at each passing:
wind gnaws the branches,

                               sounds out bone
to the hungry dogs.

We are scared that way,
           that way dice
eclipsed by a closed fist

shiver like dead leaves

                        before they're tossed.

IV.

Someone sings a love song

to the very river that drowned my brother three   years   back.

The seasons are vermin
sneaking solemn through the years.

He looks like you
            so say.
He is quite handsome
so say

softly. I am scared of the river which drowns each day,
scared of the thirst that draws me to it —
                                    and to be scared is a sign

of a certain type of respect.
I remember him the way one might lay a wall.

Memorized him,
the way one might burn a field.

V.

It was not my brother, it was me

who drowns to return again and again.
                                    Each night

brings the same dream and each morning
                          over coffee at the salina, someone new
whines to play with the new toy of it.

          To crack its shell and leave me
with the mess.

Make symbol out of jack   shit.   Friend, maybe dreams
speak plain, maybe they mean exactly what they mean.

Every night a man drowns, somewhere.

But no —
please,
go on,

tell me how a body
of water   can be unknown, how dying
is the one slow matter
reserved for the living.

How anyone can have the idea of a brother
                                    to lose.

VI.

The corpse wood drying in the orchard does not mourn the corpse wood,
it mourns
>> the ungathered fruit.

Of temperature and nothing
>> more,
>> of the river's longing

for whatever touches it: a wavering;
a body to orient oneself by.

(Who would carry a candle through the night?)

>> Beneath this bee-stung
>> swollen sort of moon;
the clouds sop up the bloat of

all that rotten   yellow light.

VII.

(Leave knocking to the ghosts).

(Force is the virtue
that makes god perfect).

VIII.

I do have a brother, did,
do. All the cars

in smalltownburgville are red
                              and idling
on the torn-up baseball field.

Down
        at the salt ponds
                    the children night-fish

and gig frogs with stolen .22s.

But my brother, my brother
was not supposed to be
my brother. There are no houses large enough

for more than one child in this town. The womb
has been spooned empty   as the hills.

Let me put it bluntly:
luck's the technique
we use to organize

                              each of our petty
(or did I mean pretty) losses.

IX.

                          You mustn't let it breathe.

Out the chimney whispers the star absent secret, smoke.
          It is expected
that I should be the one
to scatter the two chipped plates, to place

the unwashed silver
upon the table the way the river would
place detritus upon the banks.

Soon it will be time
to hold the bell
firmly; to tug at its arm and pull

out its one dim word again

and again: bruise.

X.

Say it in his voice, say it
      in a voice that breaks the dirt.

For thirty-six years the smalltownburgville
mining outfit yanked gypsum like bad teeth
                      from the hills

          and when they were done,
they left. Simple.

Now, the ground — thin
roof to the grave of each homestead.

The unfertile soil,
a reason why I have no brother. So point
and tell me
that's where he is buried,
                caught

between dirt
and dirt, as if he were to be reborn
each morning from the shafts

(or the collapsed
hills). Not even the dead

rest in fine fettle tonight.

Please, whisper it to me.
Make it ring
until it sounds out god

through the trees,
the urns,
an empty womb,

any hollow place could be a cocoon —
any place will do.

XI.

The trees bow
        at the waists and
break to the snow. A field of toothpicks

        stuck
in a pillow.

Just the season molting.

He's trampling the crowns
of the oaks beneath his boots.

He's hunting with a pistol.
Snow cries
through the planks hunched
     over the brandy pit;

      the snow chills it. Pass the handle,

have a pull. Fire;

      what chars the day
also bursts the night.

A toast:

XII.

The night is an ocean. The night is
an ocean. The night is an ocean and
we're heavy at the bottom.

Cheers.

He once said to me
if you buy the bullets, we can
use my gun.

So (what could you) say (to that)?

(Cheers).

XIII.

Don't kid yourself,

we're all on our way to leaving

or to being left —

annul salt from hill; shell

cracked
       like hammer to nut.

In the basement, he dug a pit
              to break chestnuts,
to separate skin
from meat.

Climb through the window
that is the entrance into the potato cellar;

wait.

Storage,
the politics of farming;

lord high god almighty

       judges us by what we can keep and for how long we keep it.

Virtue, vice,   the body
                  is a vessel for action.

Most legends say man is made   of a combination
of something

from the earth   and labor.

It's time to shut your trap,
                (please, please,   please,   stop talking) please.

XIV.

Penny the tracks or cap them —

      the train route splits the town open
and doesn't stop there.

Toot.
      Toot.

          Toot. Everyone's daughter
is named after one kind of alcohol
or another.
Everyone's son
is getting intimate with violence.

How can anyone ask
why do you still imagine you ever had a brother?

And still, everyone does.

Copper pancakes
litter the railway ties —

when the train comes through,
it's too loud to hear the caps pop against the treads;

      you know what's happened by what's left:

scorch marks; ash moons stuttering in a row.

XV.

An elegy

is an act of love, even
                    if for no one in particular.

Of a natural
                    moral
                                order, my brother

would ask

What does a romantic do in an unromantic age?

Kill themselves,
(he) I reckon.

XVI.

It's a way of making sense out of what you can't.

Without a pattern,

the sky is barren. Without names, the constellations

are no more
than chalk dust sitting
stubborn on the blackboard.

What if that isn't a lesson   dangling above us, if it's

the moon as we see it, rippling up
                     from under the water.

XVII.

Looking down on the valley, the hawks are
                grackles are pigeons
                are motes of dust circling
the drain of sunlight.

                All the mineral that's mined
but can't be sold, we call that gangue.

Everything elliptical makes a spiraling sense.

We know how it ends because it's also
                how it starts;

which is why the planets tread out
their courses, why everyone's favorite beer is
whatever is on sale that night at the smalltownburgville
grocery and tackle.

My brother
could be any miscarried baby.
With the right timing, I could have been every unborn child

(which I believe
            I might have liked).

Instead, I forsake dusk to listen

for the gas generators oscillating, the static
between stations on the radio, the insects drowning
in the creek; it's as close as it comes

to the music of the spheres or whatever such useless decoration.

XVIII.

Every fire should not be
       burning cleanly. A romantic dinner:

pasta knotted like the wet hair of a drowned woman;

      the wine, red as dwarf stars.

                        Romance is not well
suited for this town.

I once watched my brother burn his love letters
one person at a time. And then
again   another time,

so I suppose there are no lovers
in smalltownburgville or even

out past the field line   where the cities begin.

              This town is the gap between
the right to a thing
and the ability to get it.

XIX.

Taste salt, lick the edges of the table
or toss it up
over your shoulder.

Your brothers are not your brothers.

                                                The salt is snow
come early this year. Apples clutter
the orchard floor, roll down the incline and gutter
at the hillfoot —

the difference between want and need rots sweet as shade.

The breeze collects and carts the desire,
                                          the breeze disappoints.

XX.

On the side
    of each road, there is a dog

chewing on whatever animal has been left there.

In the forest, the trees cry their leaves
until they stand there, rocking naked in the wind.

    Brother for lack of compass,
brother for lack.

XXI.

Standing patiently, a suit
in each black closet. A child in each
empty room. A body behind each curtained
tub.

                                       Squint.

Sorry, no, quarantine that to   my black closet,
                                 my unfurnished room,
                                    my clawed bath.

My unshaped form.

You are haunting the world
with your wild misperceptions   so say.

I was born out of a union of misfortune and sincerity.

Your brother was a suicide   so say
                                  forget him.

I am mourning;

all the universe   and farther impatiently
paces — planets
tread their ecliptics until even
night wears thin,

which is to say,
                                bullshit
(so say).

XXII.

Which is, to say,   desperation,
in so many words.

Brother: prescribed fire,

the brother is the smoke and the smoke
is the air
and the air

is stark, it hangs too long

like tinsel,
or criminal,
or a pall

to drape across the town.

Everything's about logic,
you can trust in that:
                              to burn the forest to keep it

from burning, to excavate mammoth bone

                              from junkyard,

drown the name to muzzle ourselves.

XXIII.

I have confused myself. It's not me,

no. No brother, no

brother —
what difference would it make now?

We misrepresent ourselves
one word at a time
                        as we learn the limits of language.

The rivers hide the dead, they nod the currents forward.

                                        Look: here,
if I were sentimental, you wouldn't understand me

but if I spoke plainly, you would think me simple.

So — no, I did
        have a brother and he was killed
at war, maybe
so I write:

My brother was killed in the war

to make you believe it,
if momentarily.

And when I say, I am afraid to come out of mourning, laugh.

Yes, my brother was killed in the recent war.
Yes, my brother was a suicide. Yes,

        the ghosts have grown bored of visiting us.

XXIV.

Queen anne's lace overtakes the gardens and ditches
of smalltownburgville. From bloom

                          comes patience
and the reward for patience

                          is waiting, is deaf stalks,

blind potatoes, is unharvested

                  loss (keep

      repeating the word   until it takes

root, grows branches, blooms).

I try to carve your face from out of the mud
but it turns back to mud.

So instead I carved out a hole and then closed it up.

My hands are covered in your face.

Brother was a farmer
with two black thumbs, a breeder of Siamese cats

who refused to work with females, a bulimic sin eater,
allergic to gluten;

which is my way of saying: he was never
(anywhere) anyone (anymore).

RELAMENT

It comes back with a different face, similar but not quite the same.
She smells like daisies instead of sunflowers or he combs his beard

and you smile when he says *all y'all*
where the he-before-he would say *as usual buddy,*
writing names on water.

They return and we occupy

ourselves; instead of asking *why continue*
to care we ask: *who* cares. In these chambers, these lungs
and hearts and marrowed hallways, we stumble, pass out,

wake someplace we don't quite remember. Drab walls
decorated with velvet paintings of obama, ronald reagan, j.f.k.
Who cares. The skull is the patio umbrella

where we smoke in the shade and call it thought.

Cough. Who *cares.* We're all bones lashed together with tendons; all body.
We confuse the routine of breathing

for life. Those that want to hurt you are already hurting; what I mean
by saying *I want to hurt you*

is that I don't want to be alone in this.

And so we move towards brightness or beauty or whatever it's called.

Once we reach it, that's all we do: we touch it and we're burnt or we aren't

and we move on. Why haven't you killed yourself yet? Don't ask
WHAT'S IT ALL MEAN; the question answers: it is *all*
mean. Comprehension violates. Lovers weed the landscape;

yet we waste cities trying to get it right. Beauty is just a prettier type of terror and treating people well is a matter completely separate from love. So we visit

your intentions, leave flowers, piss on the side of the house,
compose our eulogies that begin with "Shit" and end

with someone else pulling us off the stage
and offering us a drink and a handkerchief,
asking us to keep it. This is love; we know it is

because we've felt it before: love *is* replaceable. And the act
of replacing is heavy, like a whole ton of tons. Kill yourself.

Trust me. When I killed myself, it was totally awesome, dude.

Angels cried, all my lovers wailed at once, the world shook;
everyone cried forever and that
was the end of it all for everyone. So what are you waiting for? *Who*

cares. If you think you can't take life anymore, you're wrong.
And we're going to hurt you

because without enemies, what use are friends?
When the ocean bleeds, people put on their floaties and swim. We bleed

and we pretend it's important.

Our pain amounts to the space separating one paren
from the other. (Who cares).

When the barista asks how's it going he means state your order.

Tell him your life story and wait for the cops to show
or tell him what you want
and he'll make it for you.

You say you want lovers but you've already had plenty.

You say you want to keep them, then why haven't you? Even death is no excuse.

Die-diedy-die. *Whoooooooooo* cares? We want to be alone, together. Tell me

things will be
alright and mean it.

I meant, be mean with it. Good (g — double o — d) is alive and well;

without it evil wouldn't appeal. We're suspicious of joy
and we renounce any beauty
that we can't embody or possess.

I can't speak for myself, but we can

say that we want to hurt you

because we hurt. And after, we can draw us towards us
and make it better; everything is smaller than it appears. Who cares? No,

really, who cares? It's not a difficult question to answer.

This is the tornado of sighs and it's boring.

Our hearts are terrible places to live;

our souls too —
                   achoo.

lament for an american werewolf in london

David (bluuuuuuue moooooooon, wet moon), I was done
writing letters to all the women I loved
long before I started. Dear O——. Oh, dear.

The permanence of the word terrifies me. So I request
you do this; make a practice of being wrong

(if just to protect yourself). Try it with strangers, friends,
with your coworkers or your teachers. Do it until you can't

connect what you do
with who

you are. When your friends
tell you to kill yourself, don't. Go ice skating instead.

Eat some popcorn; gnaw the kernels. Chew ice.

David, wolf, I tell you this to keep you alive, to keep you

committing your accidental crimes
(I am too late late late late late

late). They say kill yourself
and they're wrong, you know. Ruin can be a comfort; slip down

into it like you would an old suit. Say you lived your life

as an example for others to avoid. David, we can't help who we hurt.

Or wait, we can.

lament for the incredible shrinking man

Scott, in unison or union

we are an undersized canvas,
the width and height

of a postage stamp which
a mouse might use
to mail a letter saying

please write soon,
it is lonesome here

if there were a mouse post

or mice could print script
with such clumsy paws.

I married a girl, Scott, painted her,

flayed her portrait from the frame
and stared at the wooden box that was her face.

For men as small as us, that sort of thing's routine, I'm sure.

I hung her on the refrigerator with alphabet magnets.
We are so little, you and I, we are tiny idiots.

As the canvas gets smaller
its appetite for detail grows infinitesimally.

At this height, we could build a house

out of rat bones and decorate it with ashes.

We could pray to the miniature gods
not to be eaten by the mice. We could
feed ourselves to them.

to paint it closed, to hammer it shut

Without the nail, the tooth. Each sad truth comes like a cavity from out the unexpected — now pull; or drill. A hole is a place that is meant to be (filled) and bad and badly, things will always get better than they currently are. But no, not yet. So take off your necklace (last), your panties (first). I hoped for one last chance to make things worse; please, tell me how. We can touch our way out of anything; it's a cinch — pull back your hair, rest your neck here, against. Close your eyes. I have softened all of the *againsts*; I have made them soft for you. Or you. Or her. (Or me.)

lament for the mother of tears

To the horse,
the foal, to the miner, the coal, to you,
your tears

which are as much yours as they are
their own. Protect them; shed them anywhere

for anything. Leave your children on your cheeks,
on handkerchiefs, leave them in the endless streets

to raise themselves. Sink the cities with your sadness

or with your joy. Either way: your children make a celebration
out of the this-is-too-too-much-to-handle.

We've sugared the skulls in preparation. We've slung our skeletons
across our backs; now this is a party. Hooray.

Tonight's the night for those intimate
deaths (our secret reliefs) where we surprise ourselves

by saying, *finally, they are finally dead*.

Because watching is all there is
to do and it is too-too-much

for us to do and hospitals are terrible places. Logistics
are the doldrums and waiting
is worse. Darling mother,

each new day is its own unique tragedy, with the sun falling
or the birds rising or the graves leveling or whatever.

All I have left is the ridiculous; thirty-seven dollars and some odd cents
in pennies, nickels, and dimes. But this doesn't concern you; mother, you

were never a woman, you were a piece of red silk
caught in a fire. Mother, the house collapsed around you
while you accused everyone of everything

and I've been embarrassed for so long that I can no longer remember

why. Mother, darling mother, it has become more
and more difficult to differentiate sorrow

from that other thing I think there is.

lament for the blob

I spat into the night and called it a star;
and worse,

I wished on it. After, whatever fell,
even the coffin tumbling into the earth

like a coin into a (fare and fare)well, carried my heart with it.

What we need so rarely comes to us
and when it does

it is always tailed by another dull desire.

Let's embrace tragedy for the truth of it.
When you found yourself

stuck here, you held
onto the first hand that touched you

and like a stray, you brought it in for warmth.

But it didn't stay and each body after

taught the intimacy of hunger and each felt
colder than the previous. All the myths are lies. All we have
is loss and we want to keep it

for as long as we can.

I'm terrified to think anyone could care for me so let me lie (with) to you.

Everything will be ok. Tender this voice
as payment: everything will be ok.

how not to be lonely

When the ocean licks its black lips white, feed yourself to it.
Let the currents lap you down to bone: to wreck, to wrack.

The gut is the home of any body — what we accept,
what we hold inside, is held

in that spot. The sea's fat belly swarms
with impossible skeletons:

lanterns of lamina,
foils devoid of fins or tails or hungers,

leviathan ribs shivering the melody of drift —

join them; another barnacled xylophone
to wave amongst the dislodged scales.

From depth, the sky fills with notes in bottles;
variations of the same request, all penned in different hands.

They coruscate like dying worlds, charming
only in their distance from us — the message:
help me, I am in no condition to help myself. Sometimes

they add *I am here, but I do not know how*
to leave or *It's been so-and-so long since the world has vanished.*

From depths, no one knows how to help anyone;
it is this, this unknowing, that glimmers.

i spilled the tall bottle of red wine;
you want me to die

; so I do; but after; you want me to know that it wasn't enough; so I hang myself in your parlor next to the fine china; with twine I found in one of the kitchen drawers; but it's still not enough; I invent new ways to die; I have the first brain attack; I talk my cells into splitting up — but for good this time; every joke kills me; my death is so commonplace that the city has grown comfortable with it; death certificates are scattered everywhere; stabilizing the legs of tables and chairs; they block the drafts that would otherwise steal in beneath the doors; people read the morning death certificates instead of the paper; and I just thought to ask you *is this really necessary; do I really need to do this*; but I do not ask and I am covered in fresh wounds; round and straight; think puncture; think slash; but don't think of the guitar player; there; now you've done it; this is quite a lot so here is an interlude; here is a balloon elephant for you or your kid; here is where it ends and I tell you that someone whipped me to death; on a boat and in a jail and on a farm and in a sex dungeon and at the top of the eiffel tower and with someone holding a chair in one hand and the whip in the other; here is where I tell you how I whipped myself to death; for therapeutic and/or religious purposes; also; I was worked to death; I still may be every accidental death; my head was never found; my head was found before my torso; before my legs; my tattoos are no longer legible due to all this dying that I am doing for you; the ship is split in half and no one knows that I love my mother by looking at my bicep; and you are still not satisfied; and worse; and instead; you don't remember ever asking me to die; and you want me to prove to you how any word of this could have ever been true;

lament for the mother of darkness

Mater, dear mater, let's murder our loves (both
careful and loose) if only to resurrect them

in a thousand desperate-dumb poems. Mater, I am a monster,
and what does that make of you? O! we love to lose

our hearts (beat out little bird

and depart! depart! depart!). O mater,

kindest mater, cover your ears with your palms
and tell me that the music you hear isn't violent.

That chambered organ — broken from the start;
we believe our hearts, our own, whole (and hole) and riddled.

Open your chest and look: there, it beats at itself

like a pent-up child (thump; thump; why-are-you-

hitting-yourse— — ; thump), like my aging brother
unrestrained in his bed, crying his sorrows
until he wails himself to sleep, like oh-so many

easy analogies. I will never visit him again

and empathy is useless: I'm told that it makes no rational sense.
To align oneself with suffering — who

could be that crazy (us,
maybe — no, no maybe)? And yes.
Mater, it isn't looking good.
But I'm not really in the mood to talk of him.

So let's get back to you, to where

we can only be hurt by what we choose
to care for. I'm unprepared, mater,

to say anything more except this: it will not matter
(much, not much at all) if either of us is missed.

this is where we bite the bullet where the bullet takes our teeth and we ask for the cartridge as a memento

Were the woods to cry out, what vicious wild would scatter? Keep what you can, keep it inside and keep it quiet. The forest shushes itself at the frailest breeze and ends each year naked, with stillness in its sheets. If ever a you appeared, you would be of no comfort.

Not with the squirrel bones braided through your red hair, not with the grass in your teeth or the blood on your fur — to stay safe, stay still or play dead.

If you move, move loud, move now. If we were the wild we could leave together. Hop the train before it reaches the trestle; it's time to leave. Coal cars floating through the slick night, a chain of black violas and the burnt houses haunting the countryside will follow you into the trembling cities; it's time to leave.

Hold to that old mumpsimus of the irreparable heart because the soil doesn't hold the oaks, the roots clutch for life. If it lets go, we can kill it.

If you listen to the insects, you can hear their tiny prayers — their prayers deafen the fields.

Words fail us and we beg them not to. Chirp. Scurry.

Bury your head in my chest one last time, but deep, deeper, deeper. You must make a choice. Tell me to stay and let me hate you, tell me to leave and let me love you. Tell the insects to stop.

how not to be lonely

Mist perpetuates mists. Dense
and slow, the world cottons

whether you let it or not — fog snarls down the mountainside,

decorates the necks of sunflowers with ghost-bows
and weaves ribbons throughout the weeds.

Light honeys, drips from the branches of pines
and continues until it swallows the cities.

No one can see further than their hand can feel.

Hearts traced on bathroom mirrors
will never again come out of hiding and
steam no longer recollects how to reveal a lover's handprints

along shower tiles. This dimness continues

until touch is inseparable from sight, until any
forest, city, room could do for a place to vanish. Outside,

there could always be another outside; it's best not to let it trouble you.

With the scent of mimosas and dishwater scrubbing the air,
it seems inevitable that this could — this will, continue, indefinitely.

we have unlimited lives

In the video game you are a man with a gun

and I am a man with a gun
and our only choices
are to shoot or to walk away

or to change weapons or to drink a magic potion
or or or.

When put this way
our choices are nearly limitless, and we are
pixelated in indecision. I decide that I want you to kiss me, so I say

kiss me,

it's easy: fill the shallow of my back with your hand
and pull me towards you.

But each time you try to let go of your revolver
and reach for me, you find something else

in its place: a bazooka maybe
or a comically large knife, a rifle
or a grenade. An endless series of useless things.

In the end
the best you can do is a fist

and you move towards me
holding it outstretched.

I ask you to kiss me, *kiss me*, I ask
and ask again, pleading now,

but the question
leaves my mouth wet, unintelligible.

And my eye is already beginning to swell shut.
And I wish you would stop apologizing.

vengeful, slight winter

I will give

you two black eyes
she said

to the snowman
first & then to me

she turned & kissed my lips.

Her tongue, the stem
of a small, cheap pipe.

lament for the xenomorph

Where I was there were double doors opened
as wide as an autopsy.

And when they closed behind me I listened
to my shoes and the sidewalk and pretended
I knew what a heart felt like.

I was the man

standing in the snowstorm
wearing a clean pair of boxers
with pink hearts printed on them, calling the name

of one girl or another. This is what I thought
love would look like. This

is why I drive my car
the wrong way down
one-way streets. Why I dash my voice against cobblestone alleyways,

why I plead out from the windows of old hondas, with you
for you not to
do anything stupid. Why I panicked

when you told me you lost our baby. Oh. Wait.

No. That wasn't you (forgive me, dear alien, I get confused). You were

something else, something foreign, something
far from the fat sea that shivers ice onto this city.
Alien, blind appetite, this is natural, I suppose.

This world eats itself alive; moles know mice
best by taste,
pitcher plants fill themselves with wings,

even the elms gnaw at the light.

It's all alright (my mouth
is filled with other people's teeth).

I say with complete sincerity: I wanted
to be whelmed with tenderness

and for me, that worked out poorly
(I am hungry). Despite what you hear, we are not
what we love nor what loves us.

We are (   ) us

(alien, you should know,
my blood is acid too). Oh what, oh what,
oh what is left to do?

I give you my eyes for your face: hold them
in your hands; run.

he wears gloves to undress himself; the moon blows us kisses

; the moon tells us it's not a face at all; it says it is a bunny rabbit that practices medicine; that we were so-so vain to ever think otherwise; the moon mumbles; so maybe that's not what it says at all; and the rain turns to hail and I am happy; happy tonight; because the whiskey was terrible and no one here knows how to make ice without a knife and a shovel; the voicemail left by the moon informed me that the lithuanian word for snot is snarglys; it seems even the moon can be lonely at three a.m.; it texts me and I think it's drunk on wine again; I can tell by looking at its lips; wat r u doing cutie? can I cmme oevr?; and I know that you kissed the red from the lips; I know now; you want to be in love; so you wait for a redhead in a red dress; she arrives; she asks you; what did you expect would happen; she asks; and she keeps asking questions as she walks toward the ocean; you *say say say* to the back of her head; her face reflects the waves; her red dress is turning black and her hair is turning black and the night is turning black; the ocean curves back up and back into itself; and you can no longer separate her form from the foam; there's sand in your shoes; her red dress beaches itself on the shore; seaweed or hair; and no one is ever coming back; which I am only sorry to tell you because; I wanted to be the comfort that I am not;

lament for dr. jekyll

We have become as good as we dress; now
Henry please Henry listen listen listen

we are either (mis)tooken or (mis)taken with the grotesque.

Whoever was buried (you),
let's say we were there. We paid our respects, I spit my secret
into your coffin, and nailed it shut (all of us love in jest).

So yeah — then, me (myself)
and everyone else, we all went back to business. But what,

oh what to do? Not much for you. These days
the only decent virtues are grief and cruelty. Who is left to kiss
the blackmouthed brutes reclining against the cobblestone walls?
The answer is: all, all all. Pucker up.

This practice of living has made me sick.

The woman said she loved
me (for a while) after I pressed her like a flower
between myself and a chain link fence (our lips
are broken filaments). The wicked can take

and take for the simple sake of it and for this
they are blessed.

I can't live with myself anyway and anyway
Henry, you're dead, so let's make this quick:

with monsters, the most common question is hello
followed closely by why are you doing this.

And you already knew
the most repeated phrase is *no no, no,*

split like kindling with the edge of the tongue,
burned to ash and ember in the pit of the mouth.

And then the word is gone. Henry, what I'm saying is

I do not want to be a victim anymore.

lament for the shape

Your house abandoned you for another family.

Your family replaced you
with a decorative statue of a dog-butler
that they keep in their foyer.

Your own dog smiles at the mailman,
he wakes you at night

holding your head between his jaws (his teeth appear

from out the dreams of saws). One day,
soon, he will be brave enough to close them.

Michael, there is so much to be comfortable with
now that everything has become a threat.

We whimper through our pleasures: the flowers color,

the ocean falls into itself and rests, you sit on a park bench
reading proust. Be careful out there, Michael,

because our bodies, our bodies were

built to betray. They are not ours,
they subject us to their tortures, their needs (I wear

each indignity like a heart
or cigarettes on my sleeve) without the slightest hesitation.

The body is a blank and a blank
is something to be filled. Mask my face
beneath your fingers

so I can't see what I'm doing (what is being done).

Cover it, let me guess what's underneath.

It's time for us to have some fun; to burn down everyone
who left us alone. The list has the one name, me,

and so I am showering myself in gasoline. You should
probably do the same. And we can build new selves

out of latex or wood or paper mache (let's fill ourselves
with children's candy; let's give

everyone bats and let them have-at).
We can talk to the masks we wear. We can
expect them to listen. Michael, everyone

is so serious. Which is such a relief

because I have only ridiculous things to say.

lament for the thing

Our mistake was in the trusting; who knows
if my hound licks my face for threat or taste.

Thing, my dog has chewed bald
the tip of his tail. Here, let's start somewhere

cold and end somewhere else, someplace
colder. Blow off the noumenon and reckon on
what location translates to: not much.

We need to go; we haven't. The landscapes treat us with suspicion,
wild animals watch us slantwise.

Dear Thing, I am thinking of going to the antarctic too.

Or new york.

Love has driven me bruised and blue. I am inconsolable
and dislocated; I spin spin spin

as a result of some combination of
whisky and chagrin. Thing, I'm saying I want

to defibrillate the landscape and then fall in;
for the ground to buck or shake and swallow

me whole, except for my hand unfolding from the snow
like a daffodil. This is how we say goodbye. And this is why
you came here. To disappear.

lament for the invisible man

Plastic bags from the piggly wiggly riffle themselves

unstuck from razor wire everyday, almost whole. And
you suspected that there were no more miracles.

Bud, I didn't understand the how of vanishing, only the need. What from

or where to is as irrelevant as your unbandaged body: it's not apparent.

You could twist the neck
of the desk lamp and it still won't notice you. I thought
(I think) I wanted that too.

I'll tell you about the end: when you died
everyone saw you again. They took photographs.

Dragged a chair up to the casket and stood on it
so they could get a good shot from above the open lid. All death is funny

like the song a piano plays
when it hits a man. Funny. Keep repeating that, repeat it
until it seems true.

Best not to let it trouble you.

And no matter what I do, what I'm saying

is that I understand what you're saying.

lament for mr. hyde

I fold, I tug, then find myself
torn clean out of the picture. Can you tell the silhouette

from the man, the (be)fore from the back(ground and what
is under it). No, we were never any good

at discriminating one hell from another. A hell's a hell and still

we suffer. Or I do. Ed(ward), a word, a name;
strangers correct my own, telling me that each
fits like a suit on a duck.

Mr. Hyde, you choose what to display. I wish I had your vanity.
The damned sleep surprisingly well.

Pain is rife with connotation; and who isn't familiar with that?
I like violence because it's guileless, because

it means what it means so let's act frank.

All the gods' work amounts to little more than mischief.

Dissect miracle: the occasional hole in the hand, or a stone
that weeps, or a face-stained wall (minor crimes, after all

is said and done). Ed, I know why you drink. I drink too, to
remember; and sober,

no one I've lost seems to matter very much.

RELENT

To get rid of lice, foxes bite sheep wool and sink

into the rivers. The lice mistake their landscape,
migrate, and are set adrift. To forget grief is to unmoor it;

it is to let it unsteer itself away and far and away.
There ought to be another way

to say this *this*, this *grief*, besides

years of tears & untouched beds in untouched rooms & besides the
ripping of hair & black armbands & nights spent next to bodies &
besides lifetimes of flowers brought to certain places on certain days
& the delicate washing of the corpse & besides wrapping the body in
rosemary and placing it in the rafters & updating statuses from the
accounts of the dead & firing guns into the trees & besides reading
the last words of old letters over and over and over & breaking a name
into a stone & draping the ghost cloth in the hallway & lifting the
skirts of beds & besides and besides & and and — but

there is not. So we

run towards the falling buildings, towards the endless woods,
towards second floors and shot-up automobiles —
the direction of our fears; yes, we travel towards them

even when I do not want to.

I'm sorry for speaking for you;

but in monster movies those left alone
die and I wanted to keep you

safe but now I do not want to

ask you to travel with me any longer because I am going somewhere scary.
Instead, wait for me;

stand at the entrance to the funhouse holding sunflowers
and wearing a green batiste dress, a purple cardigan, a scarf.

Hold my hand when I return and I will love you. These ultimatums
are for us: those made

clumsydumb and helplessslow we go
(lem); and cirrus clouds shimmy across the moon, and
there's breath on a forehead (graffitied to death and back again).

It's more than ok to be scared: it is natural — you can't be fearless
and still care about the world (at best you can
only act it). To be brave is to have nothing to risk. To be

impermeable is to be disconnected from all of us shaking in the dark,
who want to feel a familiar hand in our own hand: those of us who are
vulnerable. Husk and mud and blood, to have a will is to be something

and to drink at the neighborhood bar every night
for one hundred nineteen years two months and thirty-seven seconds
is something too.

So put the shem in and sew the mouth shut with fishing line;
call it a boon; the rest is unnecessary. This was never meant to terrify;
only to comfort. If it fails, don't give up: start over. So it's true: we are

inconsequential. Electrical
wires sag between their posts and we all have friends
who lock themselves in their rooms for years on end. Elsewhere,

confused, ants tighten their spirals
past the reasonable hours of evening.

When we embrace,
a lover for example, we force them to remain

in place. Please, embrace grief,

but not for too long; it'll return to you regardless.
Fleet or flit or float — what moves, moves
(us) away. We (no, we; no: *I*) need a reprieve — some break from

the loose blossoms and unformed data hung up in the breeze.

Odd, to inhabit a place; to think it is poorer
without your presence. God is, but god is

nowhere. So why does it matter who we are
        speaking to? We are speaking. Where are you?

ABOUT THE AUTHOR

Jamison Crabtree earned his MFA in poetry as a Rogers Fellow at the University of Arizona and is currently a Black Mountain Institute PhD fellow at the University of Nevada Las Vegas. His work has appeared in *Blackbird, DIAGRAM, Hayden's Ferry Review, HOBART*, and *Thrush*, among other journals. This is his first full-length collection.

ABOUT THE ARTIST

TJ Scott is a film and television director, writer, and photographer based in Los Angeles. Recent directing work includes *Black Sails, Constantine, Copper, Gotham, Hemlock Grove, Longmire*, and *Spartacus*, among others. His direction of the critically acclaimed *Orphan Black* earned him a CSA Awards Nomination for Best Director.

Scott also wrote, directed, and produced the indie movie *Death Valley*. His previous movie *Deadliest Sea* was nominated for five Gemini Awards in Canada, including Best Movie and Director. He directed his own scripts *Mayday*, adapted from the Nelson DeMille novel, *Blacktop*, and *Legacy*, which opened the Las Vegas Film Festival. His screenplays currently being produced by others include *Tracers, Vivaldi*, and *The Secret Lives of Road Crews*.

Scott's photography book *In the Tub* — portraits of actors, recording artists, and models, all using a bathtub as a common setting — donates all profits to breast cancer research. More photographs can be seen at flickr.com/photos/tj_scott.

ABOUT THE WASHINGTON PRIZE

Jamison Crabtree's book was chosen from submissions by American and Canadian poets received January 15 through March 15, 2014. **First readers:** Barbara Anderson, Stuart Bartow, Matt Broaddus, George Drew, Michael Gossett, Elaine Handley, Erich Hintze, Amy MacLennan, Marilyn McCabe, Kathleen McCoy, Michael Mlekoday, Cat Richardson, Naftali Rottenstreich, Mary Sanders Shartle, Kodi Saylor, Kate Surles, Maria van Beuren. **Second Readers:** Carrie Bennett, Brad Richard, Jay Rogoff, Barbara Ungar. **Final Judges:** Karren Alenier, James Beall, Fred Marchant, Leslie McGrath, Nancy White

WASHINGTON PRIZE BOOKS

Nathalie F. Anderson, *Following Fred Astaire*, 1998
Michael Atkinson, *One Hundred Children Waiting for a Train*, 2001
Molly Bashaw, *The Whole Field Still Moving Inside It*, 2013
Carrie Bennett, *biography of water*, 2004
Peter Blair, *Last Heat*, 1999
John Bradley, *Love-in-Idleness: The Poetry of Roberto Zingarello*,
     1995, 2ND edition 2015
Richard Carr, *Ace*, 2008
B. K. Fischer, *St. Rage's Vault*, 2012
Ann Rae Jonas, *A Diamond Is Hard But Not Tough*, 1997
Frannie Lindsay, *Mayweed*, 2009
Richard Lyons, *Fleur Carnivore*, 2005
Fred Marchant, *Tipping Point*, 1993, 2ND edition 2013
Ron Mohring, *Survivable World*, 2003
Barbara Moore, *Farewell to the Body*, 1990
Brad Richard, *Motion Studies*, 2010
Jay Rogoff, *The Cutoff*, 1994
Prartho Sereno, *Call from Paris*, 2007, 2ND edition 2013
Enid Shomer, *Stalking the Florida Panther*, 1987
John Surowiecki, *The Hat City After Men Stopped Wearing Hats*, 2006
Miles Waggener, *Phoenix Suites*, 2002
Mike White, *How to Make a Bird with Two Hands*, 2011
Nancy White, *Sun, Moon, Salt*, 1992, 2ND edition 2010

ABOUT THE WORD WORKS

The Word Works, a nonprofit literary organization, publishes contemporary poetry and presents public programs.

Imprints include The Washington Prize, Hilary Tham Capital Collection, International Editions, and The Tenth Gate Prize. A reading period is also held in May.

Monthly, The Word Works offers free literary programs in the Chevy Chase, MD, Café Muse series, and each summer, it holds free poetry programs in Washington, D.C.'s Rock Creek Park. Annually in June, two high school students debut in the Joaquin Miller Poetry Series as winners of the Jacklyn Potter Young Poets Competition. Since 1974, Word Works programs have included: "In the Shadow of the Capitol," a symposium and archival project on the African American intellectual community in segregated Washington, D.C.; the Gunston Arts Center Poetry Series; the Poet Editor panel discussions at The Writer's Center; and Master Class workshops.

As a 501(c)3 organization, The Word Works has received awards from the National Endowment for the Arts, the National Endowment for the Humanities, the D.C. Commission on the Arts & Humanities, the Witter Bynner Foundation, Poets & Writers, The Writer's Center, Bell Atlantic, the David G. Taft Foundation, and others, including many generous private patrons.

The Word Works has established an archive of artistic and administrative materials in the Washington Writing Archive housed in the George Washington University Gelman Library. It is a member of the Council of Literary Magazines and Presses and its books are distributed by Small Press Distribution.

More information available at WordWorksBooks.org

OTHER WORD WORKS BOOKS

FROM THE HILARY THAM CAPITAL COLLECTION

Mel Belin, *Flesh That Was Chrysalis*
Doris Brody, *Judging the Distance*
Sarah Browning, *Whiskey in the Garden of Eden*
Grace Cavalieri, *Pinecrest Rest Home*
Christopher Conlon, *Gilbert and Garbo in Love*
       & *Mary Falls: Requiem for Mrs. Surratt*
Donna Denizé, *Broken like Job*
W. Perry Epes, *Nothing Happened*
Bernadette Geyer, *The Scabbard of Her Throat*
Barbara G. S. Hagerty, *Twinzilla*
James Hopkins, *Eight Pale Women*
Brandon Johnson, *Love's Skin*
Marilyn McCabe, *Perpetual Motion*
Judith McCombs, *The Habit of Fire*
James McEwen, *Snake Country*
Miles David Moore, *The Bears of Paris*
       & *Rollercoaster*
Kathi Morrison-Taylor, *By the Nest*
Michael Shaffner, *The Good Opinion of Squirrels*
Maria Terrone, *The Bodies We Were Loaned*
Hilary Tham, *Bad Names for Women*
       & *Counting*
Barbara Ungar, *Charlotte Brontë, You Ruined My Life*
       & *Immortal Medusa*
Jonathan Vaile, *Blue Cowboy*
Tera Vale Ragan, *Reading the Ground*
Rosemary Winslow, *Green Bodies*
Michele Wolf, *Immersion*
Joseph Zealberg, *Covalence*

The Tenth Gate Prize

Lisa Sewell, *Impossible Object*, 2014

International Editions

Keyne Cheshire (trans.), *Murder at Jagged Rock: A Tragedy
    by Sophocles*
Yoko Danno & James C. Hopkins, *The Blue Door*
Moshe Dor, Barbara Goldberg, Giora Leshem, eds.,
    The Stones Remember: Native Israeli Poets
Moshe Dor (Barbara Goldberg, trans.), *Scorched by the Sun*
Lee Sang (Myong-Hee Kim, trans.), *Crow's Eye View:
    The Infamy of Lee Sang, Korean Poet*
Vladimir Levchev (Henry Taylor, trans.), *Black Book of the
    Endangered Species*

Additional Titles

Karren L. Alenier, *Wandering on the Outside*
Karren L. Alenier, Hilary Tham, Miles David Moore, eds.,
    Winners: A Retrospective of the Washington Prize
Christopher Bursk, ed., *Cool Fire*
Barbara Goldberg, *Berta Broadfoot and Pepin the Short*
W.T. Pfefferle, *My Coolest Shirt*
Jacklyn Potter, Dwaine Rieves, Gary Stein, eds., *Cabin Fever:
    Poets at Joaquin Miller's Cabin*
Robert Sargent, *Aspects of a Southern Story
    & A Woman from Memphis*

CPSIA information can be obtained
at www.ICGtesting.com
Printed in the USA
FFOW05n1018170415

9 780915 380923